SHEKINAH
Speaks

Divination Poetry
for the UnBridled Woman

BY KATRINA

Copyright © 2025 by Katrina

All rights reserved. No part of this book may be reproduced or transmitted in any form or by any means, electronic or mechanical, including photocopying, recording, or by any information storage and retrieval system, without permission in writing from the publisher.

ISBN:
978-1-916529-52-6 (Paperback)
978-1-916529-61-8 (Hardback)
978-1-916529-53-3 (ebook)

Cover design by Lynda Mangoro.

The Unbound Press
www.theunboundpress.com

Hey unbound one!

Welcome to this magical book brought to you by The Unbound Press.

At The Unbound Press, we believe that when women write freely from the fullest expression of who they are, it can't help but activate a feeling of deep connection and transformation in others. When we come together, we become more and we're changing the world, one book at a time!

This book has been carefully crafted by both the author and publisher with the intention of inspiring you to move ever more deeply into who you truly are.

We hope that this book helps you to connect with your Unbound Self and that you feel called to pass it on to others who want to live a more fully expressed life.

With much love,

Nicola Humber

Founder of The Unbound Press
www.theunboundpress.com

Shekinah Speaks

Divination Poetry for the UnBridled Woman – by Katrina

This poetry is designed to move you.

To uplift you.

To heal you.

To hold you in love's warm embrace while you traverse the tides of time along the sacred journey of your unfolding heart.

Stamped with the transformative energy of the current that is now, the poetry is infused with collective healing for the perennial wound held deep within the feminine.

I hope you feel nurtured in the melody of my words, while you heed the calls of your tomorrow...

***

You are also invited to use this book as a Divination Tool: let your thumb choose a page and seek what you long to know when you get there.

*Her Intensity
Unravels Him*

– Katrina, 2015

Contents

Preface	11
Introduction	13
And Now, She Speaks...	**15**
The Black Madonna Rises Again	17
The Sacred Prostitute	19
Last Night	22
Dear Beloved	24
The Seductress	26
As A Woman	27
On His Melancholy Lips	30
Twin Love Never Dies	31
The Fabric of a Woman's Being	33
Internal Landscape	35
The Perennial Wound: A Trilogy	36
Her Murmurs Wake His Heart	43
When Love Beckons	44
The Music of Oneness	45

You, The Sculpture	47
She Will Have Your Lips	49
Battle Me	52
In Your Heart My Soul Travels	58
As She Whispers	64
Her Heart Knows	65
Bound By Devotion No More	67
You Are The Universe Embodied	68
Her Infinite Breath	69
White Witches Unite	70
She Manifests	71
She's a Faery	72
Is He Your Sun?	73
Hope's Despair: The Lineage of Lack	75
Shattered Dreams	77
When They Fly	78
I Will Not Apologise: A Woman's Pledge	80

Preface

The background noise, can you hear it?

The rhythm of Her rising: drums beating, solar flaring, wildly intoxicating call to say, *the greatest show on Earth is about to begin*.

Shekinah is back.

The very wisdom of shadow-feminine intelligence, rising in all of us, its voice is getting louder and louder.

No one, nothing, can stop it now.

The time has arrived.

Brace yourselves, hug your sisters and brothers.

She can't be stamped out any longer.

The stakes are about to get balanced.

It's time.

Katrina xo

INTRODUCTION

Have you ever had a muse? That one thing that gets your flow going, miraculously, mysteriously, deliciously?

It's phenomenal just how easily a muse connects you to your zone. That sweet wellspring of flowing creativity stamped with an expression you didn't know was yours...

This happened to me. I met my muse in the most magical of settings. And my Shekinah, my divine feminine potency, spilled forth in all her latent power, seeking to be known with no other name but this: *Shekinah*.

She's present in all of us, you know, this Shekinah.

And so, delighted by this newfound stream of power-packed expression, the deepest rumblings of my dispirited mother-daughter-sister-woman-warrior-wound stirred. She was bursting to speak.

I hope you enjoy what she has to say, whether she sings sweet musings, unravels her wounds, or, like the oracle she is, declares the sacred truth about the innate encoded sexual capacity embedded in our body-mind complex.

For her "genius at feminine intelligence lies in the encoding of every single woman, vulnerability the only key to her mystery..."

She knows. And She is in you too.

Katrina xo

This book of poetry can also be used as a Divination Tool for when you are stuck, or needing to hear words of empowerment, clarity or reprieve. For this, you simply allow your thumbs to pull the book open to where 'they' feel is 'right'. The poem that bounces out at you when the pages open is the one that will tell you everything you need to hear at that moment in time.

And Now, She Speaks...

The Black Madonna Rises Again

THE MAGDALEN: OUT FROM THE SHADOWS!

She's fierce in her vulnerability
She's strong in her compassion
She's faithful to her nature
She's devoted to her mystery

She's the Black Madonna
The sultry goddess of the underworld
Of magic and mystery
Sacred sexuality and intimacy

She knows.

She knows one's truth
She knows her power
And for that
Her presence is a snare
For unspoken fears

And they hate her
She frightens them
For she shines her light
On their shadows
On their cloaks and veils
But now:

She returns.

In all her glory and her mystery.

Ohh. She has been pained
Just for her nature
Her innate ability
She has been abused
Kept
Hurt
Tortured

To her core.

But really.
Did you think
She would not grow from this?

After all,
Her pain has always been yours!

Rise up, Black Beauties.
It's your time.
You've made it through the mist
The shadows part for you!

Come forward and claim your place.

Come forward
And know
The pure masculine?
He's been waiting for you

All along.

The Sacred Prostitute

She sees him

She knows
His darkest depths

She hears
His heart's longing

She tastes
His little-boy fear

She touches
His desperate soul

She feels
His aching thirst

To be met

Would he to
Trust her

His sultry shadows
She would seduce
Out of the
Recesses of his core

To merge
With her essence

She knows
Who he is
She knows
How to show him

She knows
How to carve
Out his soul
From the muddied
Scrambles of his
Messed up psyche

For her role
Is that of
Priestess;

To take a man home

To his purity
Divinity
Release him
Of the confines
Of his everyday
Imprisonment

She takes
Him to his
God-Self

As he purrs
In contentment.

She is a
Powerful wild-heart
Genius at
Feminine intelligence

She lies in the
Encoding of
Every single woman

Vulnerability –
The only key

To her mystery...

Note: A woman can only cradle a man home once she has met, unravelled and righted her own 'messed up psyche'. None of us are immune to mastering our psychology. It's just that once you've really done this inner work as a female, the intrinsic nature of this innate encoded sexual capacity – that of a 'Sacred Prostitute' – embedded in your body's intelligence – does become realised...

LAST NIGHT

I remembered that moment
When our lovemaking was so intense
That I cried gentle tears.

And you kissed one,
So softly –
As it fell down my cheek.

I've been waiting
For our love to die
So patiently.

I want it gone
From my heart
For good.

But it won't.
It continues
To blossom

Even in your absence
It grows
It's there

No one like you
To take its place
At least

A substitute
Could kill it –
Dead.

But no.
It continues.
And your eyes

My heart
Knows.
Your smile

My heart
Hears.
It is true.

I'll admit it
To you
Just this once:

I love you.

Dear Beloved

Dear Beloved:
Thank you. For,

You showed me that love is timeless.

That two people can see God through the eyes of each other.
That two people can feel God through the merging of their bodies.
That two people can become God in ecstatic moments of connection in bliss.
That two hearts can literally beat as one –

And that when this happens:
Alchemy ensues.

Through you I met
My unrealised longings.
My deepest desires
In the recesses of the undercurrents
Of my everyday mediocrity.

Through you I met
My Shekinah:
The powerful Shakti
Who now knows
That She must only
Merge Her Spirit
When She is
The Chosen One.

For only then
Can Her true Divinity
Shine through
In all its glory and wonder
And only then
Can She as the
Divine Feminine Intelligence itself
Cradle Her man home
Through the devotional service
She holds in Her Cosmic Heart;

To behold him, in
Divine Masculine Wholeness.
For that She knows,
Is Her Divine Birthright.

As a woman
Are we not born
As his oasis,
His sacred space?

As a woman
Do we not long
To hold his heart
And cup his face?

As a woman
Do we not know
To love our man
And take him home?

As a woman
Do we not know
To hold him tight
Respect his roam?

If you're a woman
Your heart sings
When you live
For his devotion.

If you're a woman
Your body shines
When you honour
All his emotions.

If you're a woman
And you long
To be this Healer
For your man.

If you're a woman
And you've waited
And he hasn't
Let you in;

Do not waste
Your precious gifts
If they cannot
Be received.

For your heart knows
If he's the one
Born to dwell
In your reprieves.

So do not waste
All your nows
When your tomorrows
He cannot crave.

Keep what's yours
Keep all your love
For its yearnings
Do not enslave…

ON HIS MELANCHOLY LIPS

As she lays in her warm shadow
Feeling safe in its embrace
She wonders of her lover
Singing grace without a face.

Her heart whispers
Her tomorrows
In its yearning faithful song
Her light cradles her forgiveness
In its trustful blatant throng.

Should she move on up
The mountain
In luscious gold terrain
Or should she cling aboard
To Grief Town
With other souls in slain?

If you know he hears your
Callings
In the shadows of the night,
Will you bellow out their wisdom
And lock him down in fright?

Her heart sings for her beloved
On his melancholy lips
And the melodies and harp strings
See her buoyantly in bliss.

Twin Love Never Dies

Under the same moon
We reside.
Along time's tide
We ride.

Under the same sun
We bask.
Until we meet;
We mask.

Under the same stars
We seek.
A love lost to:
The meek.

Where bodies melt
In light.
Casting beams
At night.

I signal in
Bated stance.
My heart stops.
I glance.

I know that
You are near.
And now there
Is no fear.

Were I to lose
You again.
Another life
We'd meet

And then.

For twin love
Never dies.
It travels to all
Your lives.

Meet me once
Again.
To love. To hold.
And then...

The Fabric of a Woman's Being

It's deep
It's mysterious.
It's unnameable
But it's real.
Men sense it,
They feel it,
They know it's there.
Many women for so long
Have remained disconnected to it.
Yet it makes for the
Fabric of their being.
It's the mystery of a woman.
A powerful potion of potential
A portal to the
Magnificence of creation.
When a woman realises her power
Nothing can stop her.

From majestic creation.
From birthing this deep mystery
From beaming
A gateway to heaven.

It's about love
Honour
Respect
Creation

Beingness.

It's about melding light
Into a tapestry of grace.
It's about knowing
Who you truly are.

No more projections
Onto movie stars, royals, saints or Mother Mary!
They are you and you are they.

It's about living with:
The Mystery in you.

INTERNAL LANDSCAPE

As the mountains collide
And the waters fall.
As the dew manifests
And the whistlers call.

I reach out for you
In lucid wake.
To clear the terrain
Of my heart's ache.

THE PERENNIAL WOUND: A TRILOGY

I. *The Wound Warrior*

Time is healing the Wound
Or is it?

That deeply embedded Shekinah Wound.

It is the sexual distortion and corruption Wound
It is the Inquisition, the Temple Demise,
The destruction of Atlantis Wound...

It is the inequality rampant today Wound
The derogatory attitude toward the female –
Bitch. Wound.

It is the silenced by rolling eyes Wound
The betrayal of an
Open-hearted gesture Wound.

It is the disregard, the massacre,
The attempt to exterminate
The sacred. Wound.

It is the Wound felt by all
Who allow themselves that one luxury:
To FEEL.

The un-numbed, the un-dumbed
But not the un-done,
Wound.

It is the well-done Wound
Of the Eternal Warrior.

It is the Wound that reopens
After every unfair exchange
After every numbed, or dumbed:
Event, interaction, experience.

Schools, clubs, councils, governments...

The Wound that knows life
That honours the living
That honours each other.

That remembers REALITY
Not DUMBED-ALITY
Not NUMBED-ALITY.

Sex without feeling
Reopens the Wound
Like it is a bad cut
That needs LOVE:
And only LOVE.
To heal.

It is the Wound that will never let go
Of the potential of tomorrow
Of the lightness of yesteryear
Of the beauty available NOW.

The Wound Knows Life
The Wound Knows Earth

The Wound Knows Mystery

And it is comfortable with this Unknown!

The Wound is relentless
In its dedication to its memory
To its trauma
To its despair.

It has held on for so long
Waiting to be shared
Amongst those willing to FEEL.

Willing to jump into the unknown
Potentials of Possibility
Without Numbed-Dumbed-Indoctrinated
Going-through-the-motions
Surviving.

The Wound says it will not leave us
Until we Realise LIVING.

Until we embrace life
Until we let the mystery in
It will remain

Hell-bent on its Perennial Wisdom
Relentless for its cause
The true Eternal Warrior.

Patiently waiting to win its war!

Unperturbed
By its many battles defeated...

The Wound waits

And strikes
Any who are brave enough to love.

Then it pounces:
It brings loss.

And says:
"Now you know what
You've been missing out on all along!

Now you feel me
And let me in
And share me with your brethren
For I cannot fight this war alone anymore..."

And so it gathers its love-worn soldiers
Spreads its brand across them well
Ensures their love is worth fighting for
For how else to rally dedicated troops?

But to promise them a tomorrow
Through giving them a taste of it
Today?

And so, the soldiers
Go out to battle
Fighting for their cause.

A cause: their love lost, gone.

The love – their drug, their addiction
That's what they're fighting for...

II. *The Divine Rebel Warrior*

But now this trooper, she stirs...
She turns to this here Wound:
Why should I fight your cause?

The love – you drew me to you!
You used it as a pawn!
To reel me in to fight
Unawares, forlorn...

This love – what's the point?
I'm tired and I'm done.
You place him right inside me
Then tear away The One.

So now I'm two halves living
Living in my Self,
Still separate from my Love, my One
Yet imprisoned on this shelf...

And yes, I pay the love forward
I gift it to the world,
But at night I still lie desolate
So what's the point of WELL?!

I'm fighting for an addiction
I don't know how to break
For it dwells daily inside of me
And takes and takes and takes...

I'm done with carrying you,
Fighting your fight no more!

Dear Wound – you're greedy and needy
Yet you pay peanuts in return!

I'm done with your harsh conditions
I demand a detailed review!
Send me what I deserve now
Otherwise take me from your crew.

I will still feel alive
Just without you day-to-day
Yes, you exist perennially,
But you no longer lead MY way!

III. *The Wound Concedes*

I'm tired of existing
It's time you all stepped down
I reward all your tomorrows
There's truly no need to frown.

It's time to let it go
All the heartache and despair
You've built a steady flow
For critical mass to care.

Step down now from the pain
Allow my gifts to you
The pain will continue its reign
But only for time's space-due.

Victory is now set
You simply did not know
Now go and tell the others
They've won and set the flow!

You stand at the Threshold
So cross it now, my hero,
You've earned your reward
So mark this time as zero…

Her Murmurs Wake His Heart

As she murmurs
Her desire
In the silence
Of the night;

Quiet whispers
Carry over
To her lover's
Warm delight

When Love Beckons

When love beckons
Heed its call
On angels' wings
Rise and fall...

The Music of Oneness

I am a harp.
As I exist,
I am a harp.

Existence is the angel
That pulls at
My heart strings

For I intimately
Feel every sound
I hear;

For I intimately
Hear everything
I see;

For I intimately
Know every symphony
I feel.

I am a harp
Existence is the angel
That plays at
My heart strings.

As she shares
Her Sacred Intimacy
With me,
Together we make
Melody that only
I can hear;

That only you
Can taste...
I am a harp.

YOU, THE SCULPTURE

I've had many heroes inspire me
To beam my light
No matter what.

That, regardless of
What life throws at you,
You just keep shining.

Because one day,
Someone's going to
Notice,

To actually need to
Bask in your light.

And adversity –

All the pain,
Suffering,
Alcohol, drugs
Diseases, trauma
Heartache –

Is your Sculptor:

Forming you into
The perfect piece
Of light manifest
That you are.

The most important lesson
Is not to judge
The technique of the
Sculptor,

We each have our own
Unique form.

What matters is the
Brilliant form
Of the infinitely
Emergent Sculpture

That is You...

SHE WILL HAVE YOUR LIPS

She will have your lips.
But will they mean the world to her
Like they did to me?

She will have your eyes.
But will she visit their darkest depths
Like the way I could?

She will have your body.
But will she receive it with grateful tenderness
In the way I did?

She will have your smile.
But will it shine in her heart
Like it did in mine?

She will have your lap.
But will it be her sanctuary
Like it was for me?

She will have your hands.
But will she behold them gratefully
Like the way I did?

She will have your laugh.
But will she hear its melody
Like the way I did?

She will have your voice.
But will it sweetly move her soul
Like it did for me?

She will have your sex.
But will you be the God in her
Like you were in me?

She will have your days.
But will she relish their treasure
In the album of her heart
As I did in mine?

She will have your conversation.
But can she swim its ocean shores
Like the way I did?

She will have your time.
But will she honour the gift it is
Like the way I did?

She will have your sweat.
But will she feel it as liquid gold
Like the way I did?

She will have your children.
But will she revel to see YOU in them
Like the way I would?

She will have your life.
But the gift of it – would she receive
Like the way I would?

Would she receive you whole?
In gratitude
In mystery
A gift of her now?

My mirror self
I am your soul
Your soul is me.

She will have your lips,
But I will have your heart.

Battle Me

All my life I fought with Me
The silly girl
Who could not see.

First came Battle Intelligence.
I shunned it away!
Asking, "What am I to do
With you every day?!"

And yet it held its ground
It fought with all its might.
I had to let it win
Exhausted of the fight.

Now together as a river
We bring life to barren lands
Across parched embers
Muddying the sands.

Then came Battle Beauty.
I said, "Please go away.
I now have Intelligence
With you I lose my say."

But Beauty fought so well
It smirked in its stance
Whispering in delight:
"May I have this dance?"

Now together, yes, we dance
We are a timeless jewel
Emanating our divinity
For that IS our fuel.

Then came Battle Bionic.
I said, "No. Now go.
With Beauty and Intelligence
You ruin this show."

"But your Spirit I must house
And how to house it well?
If you ignore the gift of me
Your Spirit cannot dwell."

So in came the Bionic.
The vehicle of my soul.
And now we all live
Together, we are whole.

Then came Battle Wisdom.
I said, "Haha. No way.
Where would you fit
Spoiling my hooray."

And yet the Wisdom forged ahead
With stamina and won.
And now we dwell in harmony
A gift born of One.

Then came Battle Knowing.
I said, "Now, what are you?
You know from the inside
Yet I haven't got a clue."

But the Knowing would not go.
It stood firmly in its place,
Lodged deeply in my core,
Leaving doubt no space.

So in came the Knowing
Exhausted, yes, it's true.
But what is worth more,
Than what you always knew?

Then came Battle Empath.
Oh boy, what a pain.
And here I saw the path,
The path of the insane.

"I cannot connect so deeply
With others every day."
"Oh, come now, you fool,
I'll show you the way."

So there I had my troop
The misfit traits of shame!
No longer was I safe
I'd left the shores of same.

And together we set sail
Happily combined
The final battle over
Rest was ours assigned.

"Hold on!" shouted Knowing
"A tsunami's up ahead!"
"A what?" I shouted weakly,
From the bottom of the bed.

And there was Battle Grief.
Roaring loudly in its stead
A tsunami of desolation
Filling me with dread.

"Now go away!" I pounded.
"You have no place in me!"
"Oh please, your fight is over,
I am the roots of your Tree!"

So Grief dwelled in my heart
A chrysalis cocooned.
Until it was ready,
We were all marooned.

Then came Battle Magic.
"Oh no, now please go."
A woman who knows Magic
Is doomed. One fateful blow.

"Oh, come now, you old fool.
I see my place in thee
With your Wisdom and Intelligence
We'll find new ways to See."

So I conceded my defeat
Thirsty for the lens
Birthing Creativity:
Restlessness made amends.

Then came Battle Light.
The Light of my Soul.
"No way. You're too bright.
This dimmer is my goal."

"Oh, come now, don't be daft.
I will shine for all to see.
With the Magic and the Empath
Do not attempt to flee."

So in came the Light.
And together we did bask
Drinking wonders of creation
From our Magic flask.

The final battle ensued
The toughest of them all
Here came Battle Love
Mmm. Time to have a ball.

Love beckoned and it gnawed.
It would not let me be,
Its weapon sheer emptiness
Bombarding me with glee.

Fighting became fruitless
I could fight no more.
The emptiness filled my days
And during the night it ROARED!

So I had to let Love in
Just for a little while
Oh, but it brought a visitor:
With Passion, Love would beguile.

A forceful flaming Warrior
A foreign one indeed!
This Passion, such a dictator
Demanding: "You take heed!"

Ooohh! I should have known to leave Love out
Not concede at all.
Now I have this Passion
A flaming whirring fireball.

With Anger, Passion's twin
What was I to do?
I had to let Love ALL in
For Knowing gave my cue.

Now all my foes are friends
And together we forge on.
Battle Me will never end
While Me is a blazing sun.

In Your Heart My Soul Travels

In your heart
My soul travels
Turning left
To then go right

Seeing beauty
Turn to wonder
With wholesome
Delicate delight.

"There's a monument!"
I shout
"Oh, it's scribed
Out to me!"

So I touch it
And I hug it
And selfie away
With glee.

"Oh, look at that
Bold tower
Looking dark
And dusty grey!"

"There lives
The Grinch
Of Bower
On Cala Lupo Bay."

"Who's that?!"
I scream in mourning
My trip
Turned to stone

"He's the Beast
Of Cala Lupo
He holds the Fort
Of Heart-Ray Rone."

"But how to
Get inter-through him?!"
I shout out
In despair

"Oh, you better
Go on your way, dear
No chance to
Melt that lair."

Down pours
The rain then,
Shattering
My joy

"Perfect timing
Doomsday
Could you not
Leave me coy?!"

"Damn it!"
I stomp with conviction
"No way
Is this the end!

I've come so far
This vixen,
That tower
Is mine to mend!"

So off I set
With passion
Aunt Agatha in
My crew

For she knows
Of love and heartache
And makes this
Grinch-kill Brew...

To market
We go roaming
Collecting what
We need

At Happy-J's Hotel
We stir
And grind
And bleed.

At midnight
At the tower
The Brew is poured
Damn swell

Out the back
Of the verandah
Is this
Awesome crazy well.

Down it
Goes the Brew
With the Full Moon
And the Chant.

Let's see
The Beast sneer now.
Drink this
And try to rant!

The Brew held
Love-drenched clovers
Scented roses
Petalled wheys

Set to yield
His bold enclosure
With power-love
And rays.

He'll be forced
To feel at once,
No more icy
Grey untamed

And then
What will he do?
Crouch down
And go insane?

So I wait
With bated breath
As the day
Comes to the fore

Oh, I know my
Grinch is pained,
But that's part of
Wanting more.

Wait. What?!
The tower turned
From dusty
Freaky sure;

To molten yellow
Gold spark
With a
Pinky-purple floor?!

Out runs
The softened Beast
Melted
By the blow

His heart
Turned to tender
His skin all
Set to glow.

So now my trip
Continues
No doom
Can kill my joy!

For I know
What is my destiny
And that Grinch
Loss to my ploy!

As She Whispers

As she whispers
In the dreamtime,
She hears mountains
Sing their song;

As she murmurs
In the moonlight,
Silent echoes
Build their throng.

Voices yearning
Their tomorrows,
Hearts strumming
To their beat;

When she craves
For her Beloved,
Will he come
Amidst the heat?

In the desert:
Storms prevail,
As her eyes
Glance out in want;

Then her body
Quivers softly,
His arrival:
Nonchalant...

Her Heart Knows

Her Heart Knows
Of her tomorrows
It knows happiness as Hell

Her heart presses
on its wisdom
Incessantly damn well.

Yet she fears of her beloved
Will he answer it
The call?

Or will he lose himself
To Noon Town
With the other morbid mell.

Her heart whispers
First in silence
Saying, "Baby, do not dwell."

For I know
Of your tomorrows
And you know I know them swell.

Now listen
When I nudge you
And stop with all the fear

If I bug you and I beg you
You must know
He is much near.

So go and play
In sunshine
Sing the love
For all to feel.

And leave me
To my business
For what I know
Is pure and real!

Bound By Devotion No More

And now I am a woman
That takes as she gives;
As guided
By the flow of her existence.
No longer bound
By the ties of devotion
That held her across time.
Who now dances passionately,
To the rhythm of her life.

You Are The Universe Embodied

A walking expression of all creation.
Ingenuity with a heartbeat.
You are an Avatar.
The myths, the legends, the superheroes
the God incarnates – they're all you.
It's time you remembered who you are.
It's time to stop sacrilege against the most sacred of sacred
– the human species.
For you are everything;
and everything is you.

Her Infinite Breath

Goddess fire
Moonlight shine;
Mystery, magic
Whisper divine.

White Witches Unite

Still waters
Deep divide.
Shallow quarters
Do not hide.

She stirs pots
With loving,
Her heart
An open gate.

She hears the
Mountains crumble.
A master
To her fate.

She Manifests

In her heart
Lies all her wishes,
Lined with
Silver and white gold.

In her smile
Lies all her wisdom,
In the contours
And the moulds.

As she dreams,
Her angels sprinkle
Glittered star dust
In the night

Making sure
All of her tomorrows
Bathe in
Wonder and delight.

She's a Faery

Starbursts Aladdin
Fireflies delight
Down the hatches batten
Her soul, a storm ignite!

IS HE YOUR SUN?

Is he your sun?

He must love you
Like the sun loves the moon.

The sun,
While she sleeps,
Shines patiently
Knowing they work together.

Night after night,
He watches her back
While she traverses
The shadows of the night.

While she shines
Her beauty and grace
Amongst the
Stars and the heavens.

He knows who she is.

He gallantly
Protects her beauty
As she conquers
The depths of darkness.

He knows
The ferocity of her power
Yet he cherishes
Her vulnerability.

He must love you
Like the sun loves the moon.

So now I ask you:
Is he your sun?

Hope's Despair: The Lineage of Lack

At first there was:

A belief in LACK
And that belief begat DOUBT
And DOUBT begat HOPE.

For how else to come up for air?!

But then HOPE begat FUTURE-FOCUS
And FUTURE-FOCUS begat EXPECTATION
And EXPECTATION begat PAIN

And PAIN begat ANXIETY

And so it was
That the Lineage of Lack
Meant HOPE and EXPECTATION
Refused to MEET...

It got worse!

HOPE begat PAST-FOCUS
And PAST-FOCUS begat NOSTALGIA
And NOSTALGIA begat PAIN

And PAIN begat DEPRESSION

Oh, and so it was
That the Lineage of Lack
Meant HOPE and NOSTALGIA
Created DESPAIR

Well, and then what happened?!

Mmm, the story goes...

Down came AWARENESS
And AWARENESS begat PRESENCE
And PRESENCE realised
That HOPE was birthed, simply as –
AN OFFSHOOT OF A BELIEF IN LACK!

Shattered Dreams

Every shattered dream
Is a doorway to transformation

Every shattered hope
Is a portal to an initiation

Every grief-stricken
Battered, beaten
Splinter of your soul

Offers a gateway
To your divinity.

Sever the shackles
To your past

Untie the reins
To your future

Ride the wave of power
Present in the now.

When They Fly

A MOTHER'S ODYSSEY

Painful silence
Overwhelms her space
A mother's ache
Her pointless grace.

Beneath her wings
They grew and flourished
Without their banter
She's undernourished.

A poetic dream
Has reached its end
To overcome this
Requires a bend.

In the tapestry of love
She's woven so near
Without whose fabric
Lies so much fear.

Her wings were closed
For her little brood
Now they're opened
For the interlude.

As she makes space
For being an elder
Her clan takes off
To develop their shelter.

Her living dream
She knows is grand
As her love extends
Across the land.

As she grows
In depth of heart
She makes her life
A work of art.

I Will Not Apologise: A Woman's Pledge

This is a poem I wrote for every time you need that kick-ass affirming power shot to validate when you will not apologise for being YOU!

I will not apologise:
For being a woman
For needing tenderness and love
Empathy and compassion;
For needing my inner space.

I will not apologise:
For needing to be heard
For needing companionship and understanding
Equanimity and equality;
For needing my inner space.

I will not apologise:
For my monthly menses
For feeling pain and exhaustion
For needing time to rest and recharge;
For needing my inner space.

I will not apologise:
For my looks
For my hair or features
For my shape or height;
For needing my inner space.

I will not apologise:
For my sense of mothering
For shouting words of encouragement
Along the soccer field
To my over-smothering and nurturing;
For needing my inner space.

I will not apologise:
For FEELING!
For expressing what hasn't been said
For crying tears of frustration
At not having been heard or understood;
For needing my inner space.

ALL OF THIS I NOW KNOW:
Thanks to my inner space...

THANKS TO MY INNER SPACE
I WILL NOT APOLOGISE FOR SO MUCH MORE:

I will not apologise:
For needing to make love
Not just have sex
For needing passion and connection;

I will not apologise:
For being connected with my heart:
MY compass – who offers me fullness and joy;
Without whom life is EMPTY.

I will not apologise:
For loving the earth
For feeling her pain
At disregard and disrespect.
For now I know:
Her pain has ALWAYS been mine.

I will not apologise:
For steering my son toward his heart
Rather than telling him
To stop crying
And be a man!

I will not apologise:
For wanting to live love in my everyday
For needing a heightened sensual experience
Even when I eat my food.

I will not apologise:
For offering a suggestion
That may lack the harshness
Of mainstream's distorted notion of 'reality'.
For I – a Goddess – WILL compassion
And I WILL NOT settle for anything less.

And I KNOW:
If I don't OWN MY POWER OF WRATH:
Where will the children of tomorrow dwell?
In a world devoid of feeling,
Devoid of love, of regard, of depth, of sensuality,
Of compassion, of empathy?
In a world called:
ZOMBIELAND...
NO WAY.
NO.

I – an expression of the
Female principle
In physical form;
A living embodiment
Of the GODDESS OF CREATION:
STEP INTO THE POWER OF MY WRATH
And say:
NO MORE!

For, with my sisters –
We rise empowered.
Awake.
And we DEMAND TO BE HEARD
ACKNOWLEDGED,
And UNDERSTOOD.
For the children of tomorrow
Depend on it.

PS: This poem is ALSO FOR MY BROTHERS who – with UTMOST COURAGE – DO NOT APOLOGISE for their INNER GODDESS = their natural experiences of COMPASSION, LOVE, NURTURING and EMOTION OVERALL!

ACKNOWLEDGEMENTS

Thank you to all women. Thank you worldwide for your sassy fierceness, authenticity, sisterhood, compassion, and sincerity. And a big thank you to my dear friend Nicole Sammut for valuing my work and inspiring me to own the process of sharing it with the world with pride and conviction.